SAVING AMERICA FROM A WOMAN'S PERSPECTIVE

BY

MICHELLE JEAN

As much as I hate to write this book I have to do it. Compassion overwhelmed me for weeks but as the weeks came and went I realize that I cannot have compassion for a nation that does not love themselves. America I do not know why I am compelled to have true love for your nation. A nation that continuously let their debt escalate without thought of their own people, without thought of the country they claim to love.

As I look back in history I think of Martin Luther King Jr. and what you America did to him. You assassinated him now you are paying homage to him by building a statue in his honour.

But this statue cannot undo what you have done and blood will forever be on your hands because each one of you helped to murder him and now you dare to honour him. What do you think the guilt of your murder will be washed away? It will never be washed away because your time is coming when you America, the new seat of the Babylonian empire will fall, crash and burn.

You murdered an innocent man, a child of God and for this there is no redemption. Remember REDEMPTION SONG BY BOB

MARLEY this song I dedicate unto you because from Africa you took us, sold us as slaves, murdered and raped us, you massacred us without thought that one day pay back will be a bitch for you and your people. Just listen to War by Bob Marley.

Let's not get it twisted I am so not threatening your nation but listen to what he said in the end about good and evil. We will win over evil and it's time you stop the crap and help yourselves because as Bob so put it **WE DON'T NEED NO MORE TROUBLE.**

You can't kill us anymore because we will no longer be enslaved by your mental bullshit.

LISTEN TO THE SONG AMERICA and weep at the worlds of another one of God's Chosen.

Yes you killed Martin Luther King but God gave us Bob Marley and his songs for us all to learn.

Duly remember these dates 1313, 2032 and 2132 now with all this said here I go and American's you can hate me all you want but the truth must be told and you will have hell to pay.

Do you honestly think the storms you are getting is it? ***Worse is yet to come for you as this book is not a saving grace for you but a saving grace for God's people and the countries that God hold dear. God is giving them time to save their economy, get their books in order before your eventual downfall.***

This is and will be the Exodus of God's people as sung by the musical messenger Robert Nesta Marley.

America fourteen trillion in debt and mounting tell me something how the hell did you let your debt escalate out of hand and now you are teeter tottering on the verge of bankruptcy. This is unbelievable. I have to say this is purposely done on your part. What the hell do you think you can continually borrow from other countries and not pay back your loan? Do you think you can continually spend what you don't have?

No I am not rubbing it in but fourteen trillion plus and growing. When does it stop and all of you realize that you cannot continue this way. Now your politicians bicker and squabble over how to solve your crisis. Each coming up with dead end solutions while the interest on your debt skyrocket and now you want to tax the poor. Hell no. How much more taxes should the poor pay before you realize that this cannot happen. Is it not bad enough that you have raped your children and grand children of their future but to continue to rape the poor.

Truth is your bully tactics has backfired and now doom and gloom looms while you continue to spend what you don't have.

Forget the hatred flag. Yes a black man is running your country so what is he any less of a man for doing so. Take down your damned hatred flag and solve the problem like civilized and educated people. Ignorance is not going to get you out of debt all it does is makes you poorer and more ignorant. It makes all of you Niggers and Niggardly.

- I know many of you are making the Obama Osama jokes
- Some of you are saying a black man have screwed America
- Aah yes the Nigger scenario's behind closed doors and amongst friends
- Some of you are saying that's what you get for putting a Nigger in office they fuck up, look at Africa

- And please anyone one of you get offended for me using nigger too damned bad because many of you including us house slaves are using these word. Some of you are so far gone from the truth that you can't see your balls before you.

AMERICA DULY NOTE A BLACK MAN DID NOT CAUSE YOU TO HAVE FOURTEEN TRILLION DOLLARS IN DEBT YOU ALL CAUSED IT UPON YOURSELVES.

None of you dare blame him because America had trillion of dollars in debt before he came along. You just gave him basket to carry water and now all of you are set to screw him in the end by saying it's his fault America is in debt. It does not work America you screwed yourselves and each one of you are to blame.

Every American is to blame for this. Yes each one of you are to blame for your fourteen trillion and counting debt load.

None of you thought of your future nor did any of you think of the future of your children.

Tell me something how are they going to pay back this debt?

What resources do you have to pay back your loan?

Currently you are broke and no longer a super power.

Many of you are defending the super power but you cannot defend it because you have a fourteen trillion dollar debt load

None of the African nations combined has this much debt load and here you can dispute me because I so do not know how much the African Nations owe but I am sure it is not fourteen trillion.

Truth is America you signed a pact with the devil by bargaining away your future as well as the future of your children, grandchildren and great grandchildren.

No you didn't.

Fourteen trillion and counting and yes I am tired of repeating this because it has become stale.

America this is your country, your people and you screwed them out of their future and now you are crying because destruction cometh.

Did no one tell you the truth about the Babylonians?

Did you not learn from Eve but then that's another story.

The book of Genesis told you about the Babylonians. It told you they are the masters of lies and deceit. Have you not learnt that you cannot win the devil on his own battlefield?

More importantly did you not read Revelations keenly?

Please read it because the lot of you think that this is WW3. It has nothing to do with WW3 but your economy. *While the devil has you fighting wars you have mounted a military debt load on their behalf.* Tell me something how much are these countries paying you to work for them?

How much more of your people must die on the behalf of them?

We have to protect our own and defend it. We are doing this in the interest of national security. Stop lying to yourselves because terror does not fly in from other countries it is so home grown. ***Look in your own damned back yard and you will see terrorist.***

Do you truly believe that these people like you? ***REMEMBER THIS IN THEIR BOOK IT SAID GOD WILL JUDGE THE GUILTY BLUE EYED.***

Do you truly believe that you can win? When you are fighting them they are dismantling your economy by putting each and every one of you further and further in debt.

Don't believe me? Well don't believe know.

Did not Revelations tell you?

Go to your bible and read Revelations. America the devil will burse your heel for now because you must be destroyed not by the hands of others but by your hands. I told you there must be an Exodus because Bob Marley told you. Jah's people must come out of your land.

Read Revelations chapter 18 and for God's people read verse 4 and come out of Babylon before it is too late. One clue to you is look at the top of the S & P because when he's done you will and the European

nations will not have a leg to stand on.

- *Your dollar will be devalued to naught because it will now be worthless*
- *People will not be able to buy food*
- *Clothes*
- *Many of you will die because the government will no longer be able to pay your health care bills*
- *No one will want your cars, land because food will not grow*
- *All that you did to Africa and it's people it will return to you and worse*
- *Revelations 18 told you*
- *Some may say this is England but it was not the English pound that I saw spiralling to zero but the American dollar*
- *It was not England that I saw the exodus in but America as your people was heading to the Canadian border for refuge*

Put it together and use the symbols in Revelations your clergy should know where to look.

COUNTRY	REPRESENTED BY
AMERICA	EAGLE
RUSSIA	BEAR
DRAGON	CHINA
LION	ETHIOPIA
ENGLAND	HARLOT/QUEEN
PERSIA, NOD, BABYLONIAN EMPIRE	IRAN, IRAQ, INDIA, SAUDIA ARABIA
ISRAEL	ISRAEL
ROME	ITALY
AFRICA	AFRICA, SOUTH AMERICA, NORTH AMERICA, INCLUDING THE CARIBBEAN
EGYPT	EGYPT BUT BECAME APART OF THE BABYLONIAN EMPIRE THROUGH ENSLAVEMENT AND THIEVERY

Piece them together now and people because China is represented by the Dragon they are not the devil because according to Revelations the Dragon which is China is the one that is going to help you.

There is no scare tactics here and please do not act like the children of the days of old. Listen and do as God tell you to do. Remember before destruction comes he send his messenger to warn you all so this time around if you don't listen then it is your fault and none of you can hold God guilty for this because he did warn you

before things meaning doom and gloom comes to pass.

America I have two (3) songs to give you the first one is by Peetah Morgan Save the World. Trust me if you don't change what is happening in America you will be doomed. Hear what he said **_if you think it's rough now just wait until tomorrow._** Yes this song was written for Jamaican's and what is happening in Jamaica but this song applies to you as well because in retrospect you are raping your children of their future.

Tired of me yet and think I am a quack well it's up to you because the first name I chose before I changed it to this title was HOW TO SAVE AMERICA WRITTEN BY A QUACK.

Before I go further I am going to give all of you the three songs. Know it and learn it. Though they were written for reason's I do not know I dedicate them unto to.

Save the World by Peetah Morgan
You need to save yourselves and if your government refuse to listen then God's people live by verse 4 and leave, come out of Babylon. Also pull up **_REDEMPTION SONG BY BOB MARLEY. LISTEN TO HIS WORDS AND_**

COME OUT OF BABYLON, ALLELUJAH COME OUT OF BABYLON BEFORE IT IS TOO LATE PLEASE. PLEASE FOR A CHANGE LISTEN TO WHAT GOD IS TRYING TO TELL YOU.

Truth Is by Duane Stephenson
What's done is done but in the end the truth will stand because there is more to come. Starvation looms, death looms and if you and the world do not take heed then more blood will be on your hands. Billionaires and millionaires will lose it all and your kingdom will be reduced to rubble.

A Better Tomorrow by Duane Stephenson
Once the storms is over you will have a better tomorrow.

SOLUTIONS TO SAVING AMERICA

China according to Revelations the Dragon must give power to the Eagle and we have established that this has to do with the economy and not Armageddon-a physical war.

Keeping up with bible prophesy you need to aid America financially but be cautioned on how much you give. Do not leave your children, your people penniless to help because as it is this is just a temporary solution until you China or America develop proper **RENEWABLE ENERGY.** I highlighted renewable energy because it was what I was given in a vision to give to the world.

What renewable energy is I do not know so please no one ask me you have to figure this out I can only give ideas and these are my ideas not God's.
China you also have to think about your future and whether you like it or not you so need to help because if America's economy crashes yours will crash big time and if your economy crashes you would have lost the Ying and Yang and the devil who is known as evil but properly death would have won and his people will have full control of the earth.

- You know the significance of the Ying and Yang. You know it represents death and the containment of death-evil.

- You know the Ying and Yang also represents life

- You know about the foundation of the universe and the creation of all life which is the Ying and Yang.

- It is the key to life

- It is also the key to spiritual life and you must know this in order to continue your journey on in life in the spiritual realm

- You know the Ying and Yang is the containment of evil and this was what Eve broke. She broke the circle by allowing evil into the garden

- You know the Ying and Yang also represent the Blue and White Nile. This is why Moses went into Egypt and until this day man do not know the truth. The Ying and Yang was what Moses took out of Egypt and brought into China and this you cannot dispute because you kept the truth until the appointed time when the true truth of creation and this universe must be revealed.

- The Ying and Yang must come home

- You know the significance of the Blue and White Nile

- You have the truth and kept it holy

- You also know that the Ying and Yang also represent the head – the crown atop Buddha's head. Meaning his hair.

I know a lot of Chinese hate black people but in truth they are hating self because it is these two nations that will lead God's people home. Not in lies and hate but in true truth and infinite trust.

Yes everything goes further but you need to do what you must so that the Babylonians do not win.

You cannot under any circumstances let death win because we the black race have messed up and we are still messing up and the white race is no different as well.

Remember Israel went a whoring and Judah followed suit meaning blacks and whites whored and disrespected God. They no longer cared that is why God took life from them and put it in a safe place where he knew it will be kept in honour and free of pollution.

You cannot deny the truth any longer because the truth is now known. Like I've said there is more to the Ying and Yang that the world do not know.

You have the key of life and you have to protect it lest this universe dies and if the universe dies then the Ying and Yang dies because the devil would have conquered. This is the reason why they went into Egypt. They had to conquer it, write books of lies and burn the books of truth but they did not know God had a greater plan. Like I have said before this was why God put Moses in Egypt and he took life out and brought it unto your nation and no one meaning the true Jews and I say Jews for a lack of a better word better yet the children of light can dispute because this is the true truth, the infinite truth that they are so scared to admit and for this they will have hell to pay because they kept their mouth shut. To my people the children of light you cannot be closed mouth anymore because destruction looms in the dark and it is a matter of time before a full scale war break out and trust me many will lose their lives unnecessarily. This you will be guilty of because you helped to prolong the lies and you are as guilty as Sin for doing so and death will be your reward because you basked in the delicacies of the Harlot and caused innocent people as well as messengers to die needlessly.

China America depend on you for technology, textile, food, you name it they depend on you.

If their economy gets downgraded further it will have a rippling effect on the world and especially you because people will not be able to buy your goods.

- The suicide rate will escalate in the country

- Many will die of hunger because they would not be able to buy food to eat

- You will not get paid because the American dollar will become worthless therefore causing other currencies to rise

- How will you pay your bills if they cannot pay you because America is your biggest customer for manufactured goods?

- How will you feed your people?

- How will you provide for them?

Hear me now and start investing in renewable energy because trust me infinitely when I tell you that the oil sands will dry up. I do not know when it will fully dry up but it is going to fully dry up.

Limitless resources of the planet

Wrong. The resources of this planet are limited. None of you are giving proper notice to the universe. None of you are looking at the distance between the earth and the sun. Let's not forget the moon. We need to seriously take a check because none of you know that the earth is shifting meaning there is no longer a natural balance with nature.

None of us know that we are being pulled closer to the sun and no matter how minute the change, it has a significant impact on the civilization upon the face of the earth.

China you have a billion plus people to oversee find ways to use your garbage to produce fuel for cars, heat your homes and businesses

- Human and animal waste (feces) how about using that for fuel

- How about developing cleaner means to produce coal and use it effectively in day to day use

- Your country consume a lot of plastic

how about recycling this plastic and make shoes, clothes-rain gear, plastic plates, cups, utensils. I know this is already being done improve on this

- Things that we wouldn't think of using plastic for do it. Be inventive but make the product safe, free of harmful chemicals and led

- Make some crazy dolls that kids would enjoy

- Make toy pianos and guitars from plastic that actually work

- The plastic bottles that we dispose of why not find a way to make beds for pets.

- Houses for pets

- We dispose of a lot of clothes how about recycling those used clothing and make funky clothing for pets, like ties, tuxedo's shirts or even pants, hats for the head

- Some of these clothing can be used to make bed linen like blankets for pets. These clothing can outline the bed.

- How about developing efficient use of solar energy but do not just use the sun but also use the moon meaning ways of using the moons rays or energy as a cooling system to cool down your country because trust me this earth is so going to get much hotter

- You make cars and so does the Japanese so develop a type of nozzle or something that can be retrofitted to all cars so that they burn less gas. Hence we are helping the environment. And Mr. Gas companies don't come after me for this. Yes you will lose money but you are prolonging the inevitable. Meaning you are prolonging your inevitable extinction. I know you have electric cars but they are so not efficient plus think of the long term drain on the electrical grid and our water supply. Hybrid cars are there but how many people can

SAVING AMERICA FROM A WOMAN'S PERSPECTIVE

afford these cars.

These are ideas and like I said I know nothing about Renewable Energy so please Mr. Economists and Scientist do not blast me okay. I know a lot of these things are being done but we need to clear up the landfills in our country and if we can use the mountains of garbage globally to do so why not.

People I do not know how long we have all I know is 1313, 2032, 2132. These are the dates I was given but 2032 is a significant date because this is date I keep getting recurring dreams about.

AND PEOPLE DO NOT PANIC BECAUSE I DID NOT SEE DOOM AND GLOOM ASSOCIATED WITH THESE DATES.

If there is doom and gloom I will see it but currently these dates are too far into the future for me to see and tell.

So far I have seen the Moon turning full red and that was 9/11

I have seen a huge moon so full that it was almost touching the ground on earth meaning you could physically touch it and that have not come to pass as yet because I so do not know what this means or what it represents

The one I cannot figure out is the GREEN and GOLD Moon in the Northeast of Canada. It was beautiful. I have never seen a moon like this before. I so do not know what it means or what it represents. If you can figure this out let me know as I am so stumped.

So China do you see where I am going with the renewable energy. You need to become future ready because if America can't pay then you will not get paid and your economy will crash and burn like America's. You will end up in the same sink hole that they are in so start developing and start selling.

Maybe these ideas do not sound appealing but you never know. Do not rely on oil to save you because it is only a matter of time before it runs out.

It could by be 2032 we see a difference and by 2132 it will all be gone. I do not know and I cannot tell anyone to buckle down and prepare for the worst because to so far the worst was not shown to me. All that was shown was renewable energy and I will harp and preach on renewable energy because it is the saving grace for the future and future generations to come.

Maybe this renewable energy will save us in the future from this comet and yes people I did see it coming whether it hits earth that is another story. Maybe it will pass by earth or come close to earth I do not know. This comet Revelations also talked about but they called it Wormwood.

It is not fake it is as real as God himself.

And people you can poke holes in the bible but the truth not the full truth is buried in there you just have to find it.

2) Donations

All American can donate $10.00 to the government of America

Most of you will be arguing about this but why. You claim to love your country prove to me that you all love America and don't want it to fall in the hands of the Babylonians.

Reclaim your birthright by letting go of the devils hand and do something to save your country.

Some of you are saying why the hell should we our government got us into this mess?

You elected these officials and now they are squabbling about your economy instead of coming up with concrete solutions as to how to fix it. And besides this is not a political game. Your debt crisis affect not only America but the global economy.

$10 dollars is not enough I know but the $10 is for the ordinary citizens to give and I know it hurts because most of your money is spent on war and the political games other countries play.

Let's put it this way all powerful country that governs by war and greed must come crashing down. Babylon did long ago but it's resurfacing not so much on the political warfront but in the economic arena.

The devil does not need weapons of mass destruction anymore. Those are outdated but don't get me wrong don't think for a minute that the devil will not use force to get what he wants. He will and he is so not afraid of doing so. Right now his war is on the economic front. Cripple a countries economy. Make them get so far in debt that they cannot pay their bills.

These countries are poor we have to do something to help some of you are saying.

Nigga who's fooling you. These countries are not poor they just know how to hide their wealth better than you.

Just as how they train their children to hate your ass trust me they will starve their people, make them go hungry just to get the job done. This is hatred you are spreading.

Go back to Genesis and America bare with me. Did Satan or the Devil not tell Eve she would not die?

Yes

Did she die?
Yes but not right away.

Lies and abomination on your part because she died immediately spiritually. That connection she no longer had with God. The freedom with God she no longer had because she became dirty. She also died physically.

Now tell me this did Eve become like Gods.

Yes because Genesis said they became like one of us knowing good and evil

Then the 640000 dollar question is if they were like gods why then did they meaning Adam and Eve have to die. God never died meaning the true and living God never died so why did they have to die?

I don't know you are saying.

Is death not a God?

No

Yes death is a God. Is it not death that takes your soul when you die? Is death not all powerful?

No

So then why did Satan tell Eve she would become like God and why did God tell Satan in Job to **"do unto Job that you will but <u>do not take his life."</u>**

You tell me because all I know is Satan is a liar

Prove to me that Satan is a liar

And no people I am so not a Satanist I am just trying to prove a point and getting too far into this so I am going to stop right here until we can have a conversation face to face because this book is about Saving America.

Stop saying Ya think.

I am sure each American can afford $10.00

No we can't

Need I remind you of how much you spend at McDonalds, Harvey's, Burger King, Appleby's, Domino's, Starbucks etc.,

Let's not forget how much you spend on Cigarette, Weed, Strong Drugs, Alcohol, Weave, Manipedi's and more including Plastic Surgeries.

Sorry people but I had to go there.

But the government

Stop with the negative thinking if you love your country that much you would do all that you can to help

What if I can't afford $10.00?

Pray sincerely that God will help America to recover from the situation it is in

All you millionaires and billionaires you can do your part to help and no the $10.00 does not apply to you because the lot of you can give more to help out your country.

America has tons of millionaires and you too can afford to donate a million or two. So do it and help out your country.

For all you billionaires I am sure you all can give a billion or two

Make that sacrifice and help because you all more than have it to give. Give what you can that means if you are a millionaire and you can only afford $25000.00 give it. Do not leave yourself broke because you have to think about tomorrow.

But the debt is fourteen trillion some of you are harping and wining about

And your point it took your country less than 100 years to rack up this mountainous debt

You all want the bigger cars, bigger houses, the expensive this and the expensive that

Hey I am so not knocking or rocking your boat because some of you have worked damned hard for your money

And no I am so not jealous so don't even think it or go there so help

It's not why should I people

This is something good you are doing

How is it good you are asking us to give up millions even billions

And your point

Let me put it this way, go back to Revelations 18 and read it then tell me what good your millions and billions will be if Revelations 18 come to pass. The lot of you will be so broke that many of you will end your life via suicide. This will be worse than the great depression.

- Remember no one will be able to buy your goods
- No high end running shoes

- No computers
- No movies-meaning American's will not be able to afford to go to the movies because they have no money to pay for their ticket
- Your designer clothing will become bargain dollar clothing
- Food will become scarce because people will not be able to buy food therefore many of the food will rot on the shelves
- Many countries will not sell to your country because you and or your country cannot afford to buy their goods
- Your government will not be able to pay its workers

- Your government cheques will not go out because your government will not be able to send them out due to lack of funds
- Medicare will not be available to the masses
- Food stamps will become a thing of the past and many who depend on food stamps will starve
- Tell me something who will afford your computers, cars, homes
- Who will want American goods now?
- People would not be able to pay for their car insurance

- Many will default on mortgage payment well the rate of default will escalate
- Suicide rate will rise
- Looting will occur
- The city will burn because people will get fed up of the high unemployment and the same thing that happened in England recently will happen in America
- There will be increased shortage of medicine
- Disease will infest the country
- Children will not be able to receive critical care medicines and operations because families will no longer be able to afford this nor will your government be able to help you
- The country will be in a state of poverty worse than Africa

Let's see the same nation that you trampled down and screwed will now become the super power because Africa and African's will wake up once they see your collapse and provide all that you can't to other nations.

In a nutshell the devil would have left your nation so poverty stricken that it will now reign and yes enslave your asses because this is what you want and no matter how you look at it you are giving it to him with the constant bickering. So what if your President is black. There is no historic landmark here because America would have come full circle home because North and South America was once a part of Africa. Well not all of North America anyway.

The oil

Will never have it because guess what you are broke

We have oil and natural gas

For how long?

Africa and the African nations have oil and you depend on them because their oil is easier to break down. Let's not forget the oil sands will dry up and you will have nothing.

If the oil sands dry up here it will dry up in Africa too

True but Africa is hot and America have a mixture of temperature so you had better develop a lot more natural gas and find ways to use the garbage that you store up at landfills to fuel your cars and heat your homes.

You don't know when the oil sands will dry up

No but 1313, 2032, and 2132 still cry out in my head especially 2032 and when the oil sands dry up what back up do you have to fuel your cars. I know you have back up but how long will those back up last because you America consume so much oil that it is unbelievable.

China has over one billion people and you consume more oil than them

All this maybe nonsense to a lot of you but think because Revelations 18 is no joke, nor is it a lie. You can change this but it is all up to you.

GIVE WITHOUT WANTING ANYTHING IN RETURN AND PLEASE DON'T BE LIKE THOSE PEOPLE THAT THOUGHT THE WORLD IS COMING TO AN END AND GIVE AWAY EVERYTHING THEY HAD. NO ONE KNOWS WHEN THE WORLD IS COMING TO AN END. SOMETHING IS GOING TO HAPPEN BUT WHEN NO ONE KNOWS NOT EVEN I BUT JUST KEEP THE DATES I HAVE GIVEN YOU IN YOUR HEAD AND DO NOT STRESS ON THEM. YOU WILL ONLY MAKE YOURSELF SICK.

Canada will buy your goods true because it would be economically vibrant for us to do so. Your goods are cheap now. Who will be zooming whom this time around?

It's not looking good for America now is it?

So to all you millionaires and billionaires I hope you have some of your money tucked away in Canada or in some of those safe havens so that when the American economy collapse you still have a leg to stand on.

I would have a house in Canada just in case you want to flee and run to some place safe.

AND PEOPLE STOP HITTING THE DAMNED PANIC BUTTON BECAUSE I KNOW THE LOT OF YOU WILL NOW STRESS. FOR WHAT I DO NOT KNOW. PLAY IT SAFE AND LOOK ABOUT YOUR FUTURE AND YOUR CHILDREN'S FUTURE IF THINGS GET A LITTLE BIT ROUGHER IN AMERICA.

Hey what about Africa and investing in companies there.

Oprah and Tyler you can make Africa or Canada your part time home.

How about doing some shows in Africa?

Oprah you can feature your school in South Africa

b) I know South Africa has a lot of Albino's that are facing ridicule and even death do a bio on this. Bring the plight of these people to the world. As blacks we cannot say the white man did this. Slavery is shoved down our throats and we say we want an apology we don't need one. Yes slavery did happen but who is killing whom. Who sold us out and who is still selling us out? We do a damned good job of this. We are blacks need to apologize for our actions because we did sell our own people and we are still doing it to this day.

Blacks you can get on my case for this and I will refer you all to the bible you hold so dear.

When are we going to shut up and put up meaning help our own?

I am not saying whites are not at fault they are and we are at fault as well because no one is looking at the role we played in this heinous act. Both races are guilty. Bring child slavery and human trafficking of young black kids to the forefront. There are nations that are guilty of this including the US. Now you have a cause do not ignore it because if you do you are telling me you condone this practice. There are also beautiful African nations feature them as well as their culture. Right now in Kenya there's an island literally rising up out of the sea show the world. It's not manmade it is an actual island how cool is that and guess what it's in Africa. God is literally showing us how land came on earth or how islands came into existence. As for you scientists that are now going to flock to Kenya like scavengers looking for dead bodies don't. I am sick and tired of you raping Africa let the island naturally rise and become the beauty God intended it to be. Kenya leave this island natural and do not let people come in and pollute it. No one knows how old Kenya is. It's older than Ethiopia I know this because Kenya was one of the original creations for which I call one of the original league of Nations for lack of a better word or analogy. You have one of the original flags meaning shield. Know the importance of this shield because it's origin is older than you think. Oprah if you so decide to feature these African nations spread out your features a bit by including other nations as well.

Tyler how about making Madea visit Africa. Man that would be hilarious. Trust me I would spend good money to see that flick. People can you imagine Madea in Africa with her attitude. Wow priceless.

Sorry people I got off track there a minute so come on American's help your economy.

All you musicians that travel and perform you are no exception to this. You all have millions in bling bling, cash, homes, luxuries that common folks like us dream of so do your part and please don't hide because a lot of you drop hundreds of thousands of dollars each year if not per month on stupidity.

No we don't

$2500+ for a pair of sock
$35000+ for a pair of underwear
$100 000+ for a custom made bed
$1 000 000+ per year for your entourages to tell you how fabulous you look
$3500+ on a pair of shoe you are only going to wear once
$ 2000+ per hour for the hair dresser and I need not mention the sex shop whether it be live or fake

Shall I continue?

Yes I know you earned it but come on now

No I would do the same thing

Hell no

Open your purse strings and give some because your country got none.

3) For all you companies that took the economic stimulus package pay it back because some of you did not need it. And whether you like it or not you are collapsing your economy. I am talking to the companies that did not need this money. Damned greedy that's what you are. All of you know that your country is being drained with debt and none of you are doing anything about it. Give the money back it's not yours. Help your country and return the money.

As for you pharmaceutical companies, oil companies, tech companies, department stores, grocery chains give some especially the pharmaceutical and oil companies. We know you are all economic giants no titans and despite what I write and how much you dislike me you can help significantly. Give some because you can. You can't live by greed because if America goes bankrupt you too will hurt significantly. Have your accountant create a new entry in on your books named American debt reduction and use it as a tax write off because I know you won't willingly give. ***And companies do not post false entries because I am entrusting that the IRS will keep diligent tabs on this and nab your asses if you try to cheat the system. You are trying to help your country not continue to rape and cheat it and yes bankrupt it even further.***

Ya you can cuss me out for this

4) Canada, England, Russia, Africa, Jamaica no not Jamaica because they are in debt up to their eye ball. They are another one that I am going to get to later but just not in this book.

Now to continue all the countries I have mentioned above and all other countries across the globe contribute to helping America even if you can only afford $50 000 please help if you can't write down some of their debt write it down. I am sure each country has a bad debt expense account. I know everyone is hurting but please do not let others send you in a panic. Do what you can not what you can't.

I know it is not simple but then why do we

have to make it hard.

Policies that the government have to live by

Excuses again

You didn't

I did

I am asking the world to help America because each economy is vital to their survival.

Oh ya world leaders throw a little extra in there for Jamaica please. You can add a couple hundred million in there by paying off some of Jamaica's debt to America.

I know I am soliciting but hey got to try and help them somehow.

You can make the cheque payable to the US government on the behalf of Jamaica's debt relief.

I know this is tacky but it's worth a try anyway. Hey you can't blame a girl for trying you would do the same thing if you were in my situation.

China I did not include you here because you are the first country I came to for help in the beginning so please do your part.

FOR EVERYONE IN THE ABOVE PLEASE DO NOT GIVE YOUR LAST PENNY. IF YOU DON'T HAVE IT TO GIVE FINANCIALLY GIVE IN CLEAN AND DECENT PRAYER. I KNOW YOU ALL HAVE BILLS TO PAY LIKE THE NEXT MAN AND YOU HAVE TO THINK ABOUT TOMORROW.

DO WHAT YOU CAN NOT WHAT YOU CAN'T AND TO ALL OF YOU THANK YOU.

PLEASE GIVE UNTIL YOU CAN'T GIVE OR AMERICA IS IN A STABLE FINANCIAL POSITION TO STAND ON ITS OWN.

Before I go further Canada you are a wonderful country but clean the mess up in your backyard. You are great at giving but your giving will become nothing and cursed if you don't help your own people. You cannot under any circumstances say you are a charity giving nation when charity does not start at home. You give hundreds of millions of dollars in aid but when it comes to your own aboriginal people you let them suffer. You cannot take care of other nations and leave your own to starve. What you are doing to these people is wrong. They did not ask to be in the situation they were forced in. You have a right and an obligation to them. Yes there are treaties in place but these treaties mean nothing when their human rights are being violated. Come on $1300.00 per day for an advisor this is highway robbery on your part as a government. You cannot rub anymore salt in the wounds of these people. You the elders of these first nations you have to do better to help your people because as it is you are not. The heart of winter is coming up and babies are sleeping on the cold ground. People do not have proper drinking water, not even toilets and you think this is good. Come on not even your children you would want this for. Canadians if the government isn't willing to do something you as a nation of people do something. Oxfam, Canadian Red Cross, The Salvation Army, Mothers Against Drunk Drivers, Habitat for Humanity, Doctors Without Borders, Rona, Lansing Build All, Canadian Tire, Walmart, Home Depot, Zellers, Sears, The Bay, Royal Bank of Canada, TD Waterhouse, Canadian Imperial Bank of Commerce, The Bank of Canada, Scotia Bank donate something to help build home for these people. Medical doctors some of you can donate a week of your time and go help these people. Canadian People some of us can buy even 1 brick and donate it to help build decent homes for these people. Come on we are living the Canadian dream and it is a pretty damned good dream compared to what we left out of so do your part to help. Forget your biases and help. These people are human beings and the majority of them are living in worse conditions than you are.

Canada I am sorry but I had to get that off my chest we cannot set the standard for giving to others and neglect our own this is not fair. Onwards I go.

5) Let's see your army

Debt load is high

Run it like a business

What

Run it like a business

If a country wants you to step in or the UN say step in whatever way it is done. I don't know because I hate violence-killing too barbaric. Well that is just my opinion and don't go up one side of me and down the other for my comment either-freedom of speech and expression.

Don't work

Sorry

As I was saying run your army like a business and have contracts

For example a country wants you to fight alongside their army

No that won't do

See the Chart I think that will explain things a lot better

War Contract with Country X	Cost in US dollars
Guns	600 000 000
Ammunition	100 000 000
Service Men 20 000	200 000 000
Service Men 10 000	100 000 000
Service Men over 20 000	300 000 000+ fees negotiable
Air Planes + maintenance	90 000 000
Fuel	65 000 000 if not provided

Food and Labour	200 000 000 +
Medical Expenses	1 billion non negotiable
Accommodations	Negotiable
Tanks	100 000 000 varies depending on how much you need
Telecommunications	50 000 000 includes wires, paper etc
Loss of Life	Priceless cannot pay
Debt to families who have lost loved ones	Priceless-You are endebted to them for life. You must pay for upkeep of family, schooling, medical expenses, groceries, mortgage, whatever is required by the family you must pay and pay for life

Do you see where I am going with this? Pricy but I know nothing about war and I so do not want to.

6) The Church

Charge them property tax. Currently America loses out on over 100 billion dollars in taxes per year. (this information taken from the internet).

America 100 billion dollars in lost revenue come on now. I am sure if you collected back taxes from each church you could knock off a couple trillion dollars in debt in one go.

So start charging the churches taxes and charge them a licensing fee of $74.00. Make the license expire every five (5) years and charge them a fee to renew their licence.

Charge them taxes on tides and offerings they collect

No on both because they will say all money collect is for tides for the poor and needy

We can't charge the church taxes

Why not?

It's not ethical some of you are saying. It is

not of God.

Neither is the church and each day they rob innocent people of their souls

__Trust me infinitely on this. God will not charge you for this nor will he hold you guilty so charge them__

Remember the bible that these preachers preach from say render onto God's that which is God and render unto Caesar that which is Caesar. The money is so not for God but for Caesar so charge them taxes.

That is wrong

- How is it wrong America and the International Community

- What does God need money for

- Does God require a Mansion

- Does God require a Jet plane

- Does God require a hefty bank account

- Does God require expensive suits

- Does God require food

- Does God require five plus wives

- Does God require unclean spirits that are raping the souls of the innocent by telling them that if they don't give 1/10 of their earnings they are robbing God

- Tell me something people how the hell can anyone rob God

Yes this is a repeat my Peeps – those of you that have read my other books

No one can rob God but they sure as hell can rob you of your soul and money and each and every day they do this by letting you drink blood and eat flesh

Nasty asses how is this of God

Voodoo working

Obeah working

Idolistic Satanist

That's what the lots of you are

Judge not lest thou be judged

I've been judged, condemned and crucified with your nastiness and vileness of abominations

SORRY I WON'T DO THIS MANY OF YOU ARE SAYING

- Then condemn yourselves and be like the children of old that did not listen to Noah.

- Be like the children of Sodom and Gomorrah that did not listen

- Be like Eve that did not listen and condemned the entire world with her lude act

See ate an apple

So what are you not eating apples?

If apples condemned Eve by her eating it why are you still eating it?

Well

Stop and none of you say you are going to stop eating apples because Eve did not eat no damned apple she got buck wild with Satan. She did the nasty and enjoyed it.

What?

She had sex with this man and this is what the church is hiding from the lot of you. She committed the carnal sin and got cast out for it.

She got caught in her act and conceived Cain

Cain got a mark from God and Cain was Adam's son

Was not Adam's son and if he was why did God say in Genesis he was going to put enmity between Satan's seed and Adam's seed. Read Genesis for exact translation. (I have read the story and it is infinitely inaccurate based on what I was shown in the past. And yes people you can dream in the past.)

Impossible

WITH GOD ALL THINGS ARE POSSIBLE YOU

KNOW THIS.

Tell me why did Cain kill Able if enmity was not there - Jealousy

God did not put a mark on Cain that is an infinite lie that was put in the bible. Cain got his father's birthmark much like many of us. Some of us are born with our father's birthmark and Cain was born with it. He was born with the mark of the beast but the church refuses to tell people this because if they did they would be admitting that the bible is a lie. Stories made up by evil men to rob you of your souls.

For all you house Nigga's yes you back biting black hypocrites that run around and say yes the bible is the truth, it is from God, it is real

For you black people that will die for the bible the lot of you should be ashamed because you are all a walking disgrace and abomination unto God.

You don't know your damned history but you will kill for the Babylonians by taking up books written by them to keep your ass enslaved. Read Psalms 1 and see what it tells you this psalms as well as Psalms 23 is the two truest Psalms of the bible.

Read it – Did it not say blessed is the man that walketh not in the council of the ungodly nor standeth in the way of sinners nor seateth at the seat of the scornful but each week the lot of you make God hold his head down in shame and disgrace because the lots of you sit in the houses of the scornful.

Woe be unto the lot of your asses because Egypt was real. Your asses were enslaved and still being enslaved because you take up books of the Babylonians and hold them in high esteem and turn around and say yes it is from God. Let me tell the lot of you something if you think the devil and his people is dicking around wait until tomorrow. Yes it's from the song save the world by Peetah Morgan. Eve did not leave Adam for him she stayed with Adam and trust me he is pissed off royally at you so keep messing around with your future.

The bible that you so revere and read was written in Egypt by your Orthodox Jews and today they sit in Israel making changes and writing new bibles. They say the book contains errors.

God can never be an error. If this book was divinely inspired it cannot contain errors or mistranslations.

Typos I can live with but never mistranslation because God cannot mistranslate or give information that is incorrect.

When it was written down errors was written

Lies and abomination on your part

You cannot write things down in error and even if you do trust me infinitely when I tell you your spirit will not let you sleep in peace you have to find that error.

This is how God works

The lot of you say if one word is taken you know the quote God will take away from your life but yet men are changing the bible and they are still living so I guess that quote is false and your book is so not of God.

- Ask you about your true history and the lot of you tell me some cockamayney story.

- Ask the lot of you what part of Africa you are from and you can't tell me

- Ask you what was your ancestral name you can't tell me

- Ask you where was the Garden of Eden and you can't tell me

- Ask you where God created man you can't tell me but yet you can quote lies that are based on watered down versions of your history and the history of other nations.

The lots of you are pathetic and no I am not taking myself out of the picture but the difference between me and you is that I know what part of Africa I came from and I know my ancestral name as well as who God truly is.

Can another nation tell you about your history?

No one can tell you about the abode of God

because it is in you

It is in each and every one of you

Tell me something blacks and whites do you truly think the Babylonians like you?

They screwed Eve by lying to her well they did not lie and let me clarify myself. The Babylonians does not know about the spiritual realm. All they can tell you about is the physical realm because they have no part and parcel with God. They are evil and their ways are evil and wicked. None will inherit God's Kingdom. NONE

They were physical beings and this is why they tell you God is ONE and I am so going to stop here because I have strayed too far again.

No one can rob God remember that.

When Jesus started to preach what was the first thing he did?

He went into the synagogues or churches and beat the money changers out of it so tell me how are you robbing God when money was not to be exchanged in churches

- Tell me something people can you buy prayer
- Can you buy your soul
- Can you buy God
- Can you buy anything of God but yet if you want special prayer you have to pay this amount
- If you want holy water which is just plain old tap water you have to pay this much for it
- If you want holy clothe you have to pay this much for it
- If you want healing you have to pay this much for it

Tell me how is this of God?

Everything you have to pay for it

- Tell me something does the money go directly to God
- Does the churches bank account get linked to God's bank account
- Does God even have a bank account number

I guess God just appear to the Bank Manager and say all of this is mine transfer it to my Swiss bank account and for your troubles here's a twenty

You are ridiculous

If I am why does Revelations say there are seven (7) churches and each one God has a bone against?
None of them are clean. None is worthy and will never be worthy because there is no RELIGION WHERE GOD RESIDES.

Tell me something is there a place reserved in God's abode for which you call heaven for Muslims, Jews, Zionist, Jehovah's Witnesses, Seventh Day Adventist, Protestants, Catholics and the sorts

There are no sections where God resides

That's a lie there are different gates and each tribe that are mentioned in Revelations will enter

So which tribe are you from?

Are you from the tribe of Dan or from the tribe of Reuben?

I am so not from any of these tribes and as I recall only 144 000 will enter and there are billions of people on the face of this planet so I guess we are all going to hell except for these chosen few.

It's not like that

What is it like because the law is the law and God cannot change the law to accommodate any of you? If he did he would be a damned liar and does not practice what he teaches and I stand on record as saying this.

God cannot lie

So why do you lie for him?

Jesus died for us

Why did he have to die and is not one of his teachings were he came to fulfill the law not to change them so why is collection still being picked up in church

Isaiah prophesied of his death

Was it the death of Jesus that Isaiah told about or was it the death of John the

Baptist?

Do you truly know the story of Jesus and why he came into being?

Ask a true Jew or Child of Light and they will tell you the infinite truth. Your bible tells you some of the truth so why not read it and anyway this is not about Jesus but saving America

None of us can buy our souls it is within us and we meaning you and me have to maintain it

And we do that by the blood of Jesus

That's just nasty. Blood is something a woman pass every 28 days. It is in our bodies and you are telling me this is what God wants. He wants you drinking blood

God does not deal in blood or sin offerings Voodoo Priests and Priestesses requires blood

Satanist require blood

Death requires blood

Tell me something if David had blood on his hands and he could not build God's temple of praise how the hell do you think you are going to get to heaven

Moses killed

Infinite lie that was told on Moses

Moses could never have killed anyone and touched life meaning carry life out of Egypt. He could have never touched the Ying and the Yang and this is the infinite truth.

No man that has touched blood can bring forth life this is impossible and some of you clergy know this but continue to spread lies upon God. When is enough enough on your part?

You all say you are of God but yet do what you are not to do and say it is of God and this is wrong.

Let me ask the lot of you something. Do you know what hell is truly all about? Have you seen hell with your spiritual eye?

I have seen hell, know what awaits the lot

of you and trust me infinitely it is not pretty.

I have said it before not even the devil I would want to go to that place so why are you condemning others to go there.

Stop lying to the people because as it is none of you and I am so not going to take myself out of the picture. None of us will see God's abode.

You cannot do wrong and expect to get right

God never, infinitely never gave any of us Religion. I can't find it anywhere in your bible where it said God said worship me in your temples and don't bring Solomon into this because he could not build God's temple of praise with the whoredom that he did. He was a nasty man and so not of God and you all know it. He was a walking cesspool of sin. Eve got kicked out for the same lude and crude act but yet God loved him for it. Who the hell do you think you are fooling? Come again with your lies of corruption.

Your mind body and soul have to be clean

and don't even look at me because I too have sinned. I was told the one that will save you "she will have to live clean." SHE not he and people especially you women do not jump up and say I am her. Meaning say you are her. I have seen the woman around the Crystal City but I have yet to see your saving grace and don't even look at me. I am still making mistakes. Don't even think of it lest I blast you.

Is God not using you?

You are still doubtful and you will chastise me, cut me down, curse me, and call me all the loony names in the book, like quack, retarded, Satan lover, and the devil.

You will say all what I have mentioned is farfetched, impossible, not even worthy of second or first glance, you will be like the children of old, and yes many of you will seek to lynch my ass well kill me so hey I will go down in history with a famous quack like Noah, hey and all the other quacks in history that you have come to acknowledge that what they said was true.

Hey I will be in good company because guess what I have delivered the message and doing what God leads me and tells me to do. Remember God always warns his people to leave out of Babylon before disaster comes. Hey I am just giving suggestions to prolong the inevitable for his children, his people to get out of Babylon.

This part of my job is done and when it is all over I will be the one sitting beside my beloved smiling down at all of you and saying I did warn you and hell is going to be a bitch for all of you who did not listen especially you stubborn and I am going to use a word from your bible "stiffnecked" black people that will go to your deaths with death.

- Just like it was for Eve so will it be for you

- Just like it was in the time of Noah so will it be for you

- Just like how it was in Sodom and Gomorrah so will it be for you

- Just as it was with the people of Egypt so will it be for you

- Just as how it was when blacks were enslaved in America, England and the Caribbean so will it be for you. No it will not be this way for you it will be worse; it will be so bad that many of you will cry out Jesus save me and there will be no Jesus to save you.

Many of you will cry, wail, ball like a bitch and say My God, My God why have you forsaken me just like David in the Psalms but none of you will be saved because none of you can see that you are the ones to forsake God and just as how our ancestors did not listen you are not listening so endure the pain and don't cry because each one of us gave our souls over to sin.

Many of you are saying that's a lie I did not give myself over to sin.

Yes you did

- You all believe in the Babylonian way of doing things
- The blood sacrifices
- The walking on God's holy ground with your shoes
- Do you walk in your own house with your filthy shoes so why are you

walking in churches with your filthy shoes? Like I have said before you give your homes more respect than you give God.

- How many of you have ATM Machines in your churches
- How many ATM Machines are located close to your church
- How many of your churches now take all Major Credit Cards
- So with all this said how is the church and any sub groups of religious distinction be of God?
- How many of you mock God by saying that you are in the spirit and then start speaking in the devils tongue
- Know this NONE of you speak the ancient language of God
- How many of your churches put up on monitors the pillars of faith and let you read "if you do not give the church 1/10 of your earnings you are robbing God?"
- So tell me now how is the church and all that they do is of God
- The church is a bank, a business and do not represent God
- The church is a MONEY MAKING ORGANIZATION that rob you of your hard earned money

- It's also **ROBBING CAESAR** because Caesar is not getting his taxes
- The church is robbing him and he doesn't even know it because the church hide behind God but in fact it is not God that the church is hiding behind but the Devil
- Doesn't say much for you and your belief system does it
- Think I make no sense read your bible because some of the truth is in there and because some of the truth is in there and you know it does not guarantee any of you a place in God's abode because the lot of you believe in blood sacrifice as well as believe God died for your sins
- Tell me something and I will ask this over and over again how can the God that created the universe, designed it and made his angels bring it to life die
- God dies but his angels and man did not die what sense does that make

Think because all that you have been taught is a lie

TO YOU CHURCHES THAT WILL NOW DISCREDIT ME GET A COPY OR

DOWNLOAD JEALOUSY BY MORGAN HERITAGE AS I NOW DEDICATE THIS SONG TO YOU BECAUSE JEALOUSY AND BAD MIND IS GOING TO PLAY AND BURN YOU.

DOES ANY OF YOU KNOW HOW HARD GOD HAS TRIED AND YOU HAVE DONE NOTHING BUT DISCREDIT HIM

ALL THAT HE HAS DONE TO PROTECT YOU AND YOUR LIFE YOU HAVE SHOT HIM DOWN AND GIVEN HIM PISS TO DRINK FOR WATER

WHY?

GOD DON'T STOP YOU FROM HAVING YOUR MONEY BUT TAKE IT OUT OF THE CHURCH AND PAY YOUR DUES

YOU COLLECT THE MONEY PAY YOUR DUES THIS IS THE GODLY THING TO DO

We are still living so why tell the people God is dead?

THE QUESTION I NOW POSE TO YOU IS WHY ARE YOU STEALING FROM GOD AND CAESAR?

IS NOT ONE OF THE TEN COMMANDMENTS THOU SHALT NOT STEAL?

Pay your taxes and if any of you bicker I hope and pray that God turns your own evil ways back on you but this time make it as the pit that is in hell that is designed and crafted for all wicked and evil people

That's not right you say, well neither are you

Why do you still have the sun and the moon at your finger tips?

Why are you still breathing?

Well I am so not going to listen to you. Honey it is so up to you because I have done my job. I am not coming to you in the name of no one. I do not claim to be so I so don't care if you don't believe me because belief will never get any of you into God's abode.

KNOWLEDGE IS THE KEY so keep your belief. It can't help nor save me. I have knowledge and that's all I need because God gave me the gift of knowledge and it is by knowledge his knowledge that I and the children of light will get into his abode.

None of you can tell me crap anymore because none of you truly know God. God never gave us dirty churches to worship in so why are we dishonouring him?

Why do we give honour to God in churches that was build for the devil?

My church is not of the devil

Oh no then tell me this why are you still wearing shoes in church? Did God not tell Moses to take off his shoe for the place he is standing on is holy ground?

Do you not sing this song on Sundays during church service?

None of you love God because if you did you would respect his holy ground so tell me now how are you of God?
Render your heart and not your garment

Perfect take a bow, clap now sit your ass down because all your hearts are corrupt and nasty.

America has a debt load of 14 trillion plus

and not one of you would say I am going to help. You come up with all the excuses in the book not to help.

- I pay my taxes

- Why should I help?

- What has my country ever done for me

- Refugees live better than me

- My country does not care about me

Damned liar

Do you not get food stamps every month no matter how small it is?

Do you not have a job no matter how lousy it is?

I know some of you don't have jobs

In Canada does some of us not get child tax credit, GST cheques and some of us can't wait to get these

Hey Canadians you too can send the

RECEIVER GENERAL FOR CANADA $5 OR $10 DOLLARS TO PAY DOWN ITS NATIONAL DEBT

BAA YOU SAY I WOULD RATHER HELP MY PROVINCE WELL SEND THE MONEY AND MAKE IT PAYABLE TO THE CITY OF TORONTO, OR THE PROVINCE OF QUEBEC, OR WHICH EVER CITY IN THE PROVINCE YOU WANT TO MAKE THE CHEQUE PAYABLE TO.

JAMAICANS YOU CAN HELP JAMAICA BY SENDING A CHEQUE TO THE US GOVERNMENT OF THE BEHALF OF JAMAICA TO PAY BACK ITS LOAN TO THEM. HEY AMERICA THIS IS MONEY COMING IN SO ACCEPT THE CHEQUES OR MONEY ORDER. DO NOT SEND THE MONEY DIRECTLY TO THE JAMAICAN GOVERNMENT. JAMAICA NEED TO CLEAN ITSELF UP TOO BECAUSE DISASTER IS HEADING THERE WAY AND THEY DON'T EVEN KNOW IT.

MONEY ORDERS ARE THE WAY TO GO PEOPLE. I KNOW THERE IS A FEE ASSOCIATED WITH IT BUT THE BANKS HAVE TO MAKE A CUT TOO THEY HAVE PEOPLE WORKING FOR THEM.

Onwards we go. The fact is the little that we get help and none of us can deny this and I know the system sometimes stink because the written language is so damned confusing and some of the people at the other end of the line are misinformed.

Do you not have freedom of speech?

Do you not tell your President and Prime Ministers they are doing a shitty job?

Do you not call him every racial name in the book?

You do this in your homes on television so come on don't lie

Try doing this in some other country

Every country has their problems and America is no exception but each and every one of you can help to alleviate the debt load by working together because no matter what you think of Obama he is your President and he is trying

There is nothing wrong with free Medicare. Some countries don't have it and if they do trust me the system stinks. Instead of complaining all the time be damned grateful and thankful for the little you have until you can do better.

Help your President to help you because he did not put you in this debt. He inherited it and because he is black all of you including the top of the S&P are trying to screw him.

Was it necessary for the S&P to do this? No it wasn't. Yes America has a heavy debt load and they need to do something about it before it gets worse. None of you know that this is a game by the top man at the S&P and all of you are buying into it. Get your house in order. Clean the mess up in America before it gets worse.

And America if you are playing a game when it comes to your economy it is so not funny because all that you do that is evil will come back to bite you in the ass

Remember the days of old how the people continued to do their evil and wicked acts. Today where are they? All wiped off the face of the planet earth.

It's already worse some of you are saying

Try and maybe now the angels can lift their hands up when it comes to the natural disasters that are plaguing you.

You said God does not kill

He doesn't he will commission the angels to stay your destruction that was outlined by death-sin just like he did with Haiti because Haiti was scheduled to be wiped off the face of the planet. *Do not believe me KNOW.*

Clean up America and your homes and this include your mind and body

Each of you have the power to save your country so do the little that you can and don't think because the church is there it makes it holy. It is not. It can't get you into God's abode. They too have to clean themselves up and stop messing with your souls.

People this is your life, your soul. Do not let anyone take it from you because the life you live here on earth determines where you go in the afterlife. Let no one tell you otherwise.

Stop right there and I repeat let no one tell you otherwise. No one can talk for you in the end. Read Revelations with overstanding not understanding. NO ONE.

But

I said no one.

Like I've told you there are two heavens

One is called Heaven –this you know to be God's abode

The other is call Hell

The 2 H's Helium and Hydrogen otherwise known as H2O put it together.

Hell is not pretty and you don't want to go there so if you love God. No not love God. If you truly love God do what is right and walk in his integrity.

But what you are saying is not right

No what I am saying does not conform to what you have been taught by the church, by your parents, grandparents, the bible. I do not have scrolls of men and yes it is okay to be leery because so many before me have predicted and have you believing in lies. What makes me so different? For all you know I could be the ANTI-CHRIST but you know better.

Between you me and God do you think I want to do this. Please. I ran from it just like Jonah but was told to do what God asked me to do.

Who wants to be shunned by the world?

Who wants to get visions that you cannot understand or comprehend until it happens and you say ooh that was what that vision meant.

Everyone thinks you are crazy, whacked out. Even you at times think you are crazy and whacked out. Insane for doing this but at the end of the day you have to do it no matter the cost to you. You have to do it truthfully without lies. Know this many of us get dates but the association to the dates we do not know. None of us can tell you when the world is coming to an end because we do not know. We can tell you destruction is coming but the exact date we cannot tell you. It's sad but it is reality.

I've given you three dates but I cannot tell you what they mean or represent. 2032 I know is significant because this is the date I see over and over again.

1313 to me represent December 2013 but for those that can tell time it might be something different.

Why December?

Because there is 13 months to one year and to be exact thirteen months and one day.

That makes no sense

364/28=13 exactly and the last day which is December 29 is for God. This is God's day. The day in which everything must be kept holy because on this day sins are redeemed.

And for you that say this is wrong I am not going by the Babylonian calendar because we know the Babylonians and Romans changed the system because they fear the number 13.

Hey I just hope God truly work something

out for all of you because it would be a pity to see you go under like that. You have to think about your future and what this means for yourself, your children and future generations to come.

We cannot undo some of the messes we have created but we can make sure our children and grandchildren have a better future.

Come on people we are leaving them in debt. How are they going to pay this debt back?

Tell me something how fair is this to them.

We are stressed now how about them tomorrow.

Why should they be the ones to pay off our debt?

What about their debt. This burden is too great for them. Just as how we cry they are going to cry and will feel it worse.

Come on now let Slavery end. Let our past mistakes, the mistakes of our forefathers be lessons learned. They made mistakes and in many ways whether we like it or not the bible did tell you of it but none of us are learning. We are still killing saints and using them as sacrifices unto the devil.

It is not about black and white anymore it's about humanity, everyone and our future.

I can only talk but it is so up to you.

$5.00

$10.00

$15.00

$0.25

Car washes

Bake sales

Forget the boxes in the coffee shops and do not give your pastors or anyone that comes to you for donation to America's debt relief any money.

What?

DON'T.

Get a money order from the bank and send the money in yourself. You are doing this for your country.

But they are acting on my behalf as I only have $5.00

I only have twenty five cents

Then America well the American government set up a special account with the banks so that people with twenty five cents can deposit the money. Hey each twenty five cents add up.

Aah yes the group at work that have collected money. All of you guys go to the bank.

There are over one hundred of us we all can't go

Then entrust one person to go and make sure you all get a photocopy of the money order. Take a group picture if you have to.

A NOTE TO THE PERSON THAT YOU ENTRUST TO DO THIS IF YOU SCAM THEM OR RUN AWAY OR EVEN TAKE ONE PENNY TRUST ME INFINITELY ON THIS THAT I

WILL MAKE SURE YOUR ASS NEVER SEE GOD'S ABODE. YOU WILL NEVER EVER INFINATELY NEVER GET THERE BECAUSE WITH WHAT I ASK OF YOU I KNOW GOD IS TAKING NOTE AND TRUST ME THERE WILL BE NO RESSURECTION FOR YOU. NOT EVEN YOUR BELOVED JESUS WILL HAVE A SAY WHEN I AM DONE.

I AM SO NOT MESSING AROUND. THIS IS NOT A GAME SO LOSE THE GREED OR BE ETERNALLY CUT THE HELL OFF.

TRUST ME INFINATELY ON THIS TOO NOT EVEN YOUR CHILDREN WILL INHERIT THE KINGDOM OF GOD BECAUSE I WILL STAND BEFORE GOD AND MAN AND PLEA MY CASE AND TRUST ME I WILL NOT LOSE. *THE TIME FOR DICKING AROUND IS OVER.*

AS FOR THE CHURCHES THAT IS GOING TO COME AFTER ME FOR WHAT I SAID TRUST ME GOD IS WAITING FOR THE LOT OF YOU AND YOU WILL KNOW THIS WHEN YOU START DREAMING THE MOON TURNING RED. WHEN YOU START TO SEE THIS KNOW WITHIN 3-9 MONTHS DESTRUCTION COMETH WORSE THAN A THIEF IN THE NIGHT.

CUT THE NONSENSE OUT. IF YOU ARE FOR GOD THEN BE FOR GOD IF NOT STAY THE HELL OFF HIS PATH. STOP ROBBING THE PEOPLE OF THEIR SOULS AND TEACH RIGHT. STAY THE HELL IN HELL AND MAKE SATAN CREATE A UNIVERSE AND HOME FOR YOU. TELL DEATH TO CREATE A PLANET FOR YOU AND GET THE HELL OFF EARTH WITH YOUR BULLSHIT.

SATAN NEVER CREATED THIS PLANET HE DOES NOT HAVE THE BALLS NOR THE KNOW HOW TO SO GET THE HELL OFF THIS PLANET IF YOU ARE GOING TO CONTINUE TO ROB THE PEOPLE OF THEIR SOULS.

- **WHO THE HELL ARE YOU TO ROB THEM OF THEIR SOULS.**

- **DOES ANY OF YOU KNOW WHAT HELL LOOK LIKE?**

- **DOES ANY OF YOU KNOW HOW DESOLATE THE PLACE IS**

- **DOES ANY OF YOU KNOW THE TORMENT THAT IS THERE**

- **YOU WILL WANT TO SLEEP AND**

CAN'T SLEEP

- YOU ARE CONSTANTLY WORKING WITHOUT REST

- THERE IS NO LOVE THERE

- CONSTANT FIGHTING

- BICKERING

- NOTHING REALLY GROWS THERE SO WHY ARE YOU CONDEMNING PEOPLE'S SOULS TO THERE

- THERE IS NO FREEDOM THERE

- I HAVE SEEN IT AND I DON'T WANT TO GET THERE. NOT EVEN SATAN HIMSELF I WANT TO GO THERE BUT THIS IS WHAT HE CHOSE. NO ONE SHOULD HAVE TO GO TO HELL.

- DO YOU THINK IT IS PRETTY

- DO YOU THINK YOU CAN DO ANYTHING WHEN YOU GET THERE

- YOU WILL ALL BE SATAN'S BITCHES

- **YOU THINK SLAVERY ON EARTH COMPARES TO SPIRITUAL SLAVERY**

- **STOP WHAT YOU ARE DOING BECAUSE IN YOUR BIBLE IT SAY MANY WILL RUN TO THE MOUNTAIN AND THE MOUNTAIN WILL NOT BE ABLE TO HELP YOU.**

- I know my past and the wrongs I have done because I know you will do all that you can to persecute me with your evil plans.

- I cannot fail God nor will I fail God because I do not sit at the seat of the scornful anymore.

- I do not commune with you anymore nor do I feast on the blood of the innocent

- I do not make sin offerings

- Nor do I bow down to the dead in prayer

- I do not live for you but for God and despite my wrongs or the wrongs that I still do I infinitely love God and is trying my best to clean myself up and make him truly proud of me

**KNOW WHAT THE MOUNTAIN IS BECAUSE MARTIN LUTHER KING JR AND MOSES TOLD YOU WHAT THE MOUNTAIN SIGNIFIES AND WHAT THE MOUNTAIN IS ALL ABOUT.**

Pay your taxes and do not fume because many of you make millions of dollars each year.

Put those millions now into billions

America right now the church can pay off your debt and still have money left over to give me and the citizens of America a little chum change.

And church I so don't want your DIRTY money it was just a figure of speech.

Many of you are saying no the church can't.

How many churches are there in America? Yes count the mosques and synagogues too

Now take each country across the globe and count the number of churches they have

Now add up the LOST REVENUE in property taxes and monies collected for tide and offering. Astounding isn't it?

Forget about that's another land and we can't look at the churches across the globe.

Trust me each one of them is affiliated in one way or another and remember according to them each one belongs to God so they are all connected but yet none can stand up and say ON THE BEHALF OF GOD I AM GIVING THIS MUCH TO SAVE AMERICA.

And if they do stand up people *LET NONE TELL YOU THEY ARE COLLECTING A SPECIAL OFFERING FOR AMERICA'S DEBT RELIEF*

If they ask then you will know that they or your church is so not of God

- *Watch out for the bake sales*

- *Car washes*

- *Special dinners that you have to pay for*

- *Special prayers that is associated with you bringing money or food or whatever you do*

- *Don't make them ask for special money at some later date either remember the devil is cunning and he will use some other trick to get you so be careful*

THE MONEY MUST COME FROM THE CHURCH DIRECTLY WITHOUT STRINGS ATTACHED OR COST TO ANY OF YOU.

YOU FREELY GAVE WELL YOU WERE BRAINWASHED INTO DOING IT. BUT AT ANY COST YOU FREELY GAVE SO THE CHURCH CAN FREELY GIVE 1/10 OF THEIR EARNINGS TO AMERICA TO PAY DOWN ITS DEBT.

IN RETROSPECT CHURCHES YOU SHOULD GIVE HALF BECAUSE YOU HAVE BECOME RICH OFF THE BACKBONES OF PEOPLE WITHOUT TRULY GIVING BACK.

AT THE END OF THE DAY WORLD GOVERNMENTS CHARGE THE CHURCHES TAXES BECAUSE GOD DOES NOT WANT ANYONE'S MONEY. ALL GOD SAID WAS

THAT HE REQUIRES ALL LIFE. MEANING WHEN YOU DIE YOU MUST RETURN TO HIM AND EVEN IN DEATH WE CAN'T DO THAT BECAUSE MANY OF US ARE TRAPPED AND AS WELL AS END UP IN HELL.

TRUST ME INFINITELY ON THIS GOD WILL NOT CHARGE YOU NOR WILL HE SEND DOWN DESTRUCTION UPON YOU IF YOU COLLECTED TAXES FROM CHURCHES.

CHURCHES ACT ON THE BEHALF OF THE DEVIL BECAUSE GOD IS SO NOT ASSOCIATED WITH MONEY

WHAT DOES GOD NEED MONEY FOR?

CAN GOD BUY CLOTHES OR EVEN SHOES WITH THE MONEY?

But this is the church many of you are saying. The bible said to fear God.

So fear God and live in fear.

YOU CANNOT FEAR GOD. GOD IS NOT A DAMNED BULLY. WE FEAR OUR BULLIES, THOSE THAT THREATEN US CONSTANTLY AND THIS IS WHAT THE CHURCH IS. IT IS A DAMNED BULLY BUT THEIR DAY WILL

COME AND I SO HOPE SOON.

TELL ME SOMETHING DO YOU LOVE YOUR HUSBAND OR YOUR BOYFRIEND?

YES YOU ARE SAYING

DO YOU TRULY LOVE HIM?

YES

DO YOU HAVE CHILDREN?

YES

I KNOW SOME ARE SAYING NO

FOR THE ONES THAT HAVE CHILDREN

DO YOU NOT PROTECT YOUR CHILDREN AND WOULD DO ANYTHING TO KEEP THEM SAFE?

YES

SO WHY DO YOU FEAR GOD?

IS GOD NOT DOING THE SAME THING FOR YOU?

FROM THE BEGINNING OF TIME GOD HAS BEEN DOING THIS

WHEN WE ARE WALIKING ON THE WRONG PATH DOES HE NOT TRY TO TELL US AS WELL AS PROTECT US?

YES

SO WHY FEAR HIM?

HIS PUNISHMENT IS WHAT WE FEAR

HOW DOES GOD PUNISH?

DUH THE FLOOD OF NOAH, SODOM, THE GARDEN OF EDEN

AAH YES

WHY ARE YOU LYING ON GOD?

WE ARE NOT LYING THE STORIES ARE THERE READ IT YOUR DAMNED SELF BECAUSE YOU ARE OBVIOUSLY MISINFORMED.

Keep coming

Are you done?

Are you retarded?

Are you done?

For now

AND I REPEAT WHY ARE YOU LYING ON GOD?

Am I pissing you off yet?

Yes you have pissed me off

Then stop lying on God

If God punished why would he send his messengers to save you?

- **God does not punish anyone if he did he would not tell his people to come out of Babylon**

- **If he did he would not have tried to save Eve**

- **If he did he would not have tried to save the people of Noah**

- If he did he would not have tried to save the people of Sodom and Gomorrah

- *More importantly if he did he would not be trying to save you*

We are the ones to do things that are not of God and when we fall on our faces we blame the devil, we blame God, everything on the face of the planet we blame but none blame self. We cannot nor do we take responsibility for our own actions.

- We have failed God not God fail us

- We have failed our country not our country fail us

- We have failed our children not our children fail us

- We have failed self not self fail us

Not of God is it?

Does God not make the sun and the moon to shine upon the good and bad so why can't the bad extend a helping hand and do something good.

If God hurt and punish why is the sun and the moon still in existence?

How come we drink water and still breathe air?

Like I said do not look at me because I too make mistakes and still making them and not because I was told to write a book and still writing books does it make me holy?

Rub me the wrong way as see if I don't use fool languages in your face. Meaning I will cuss you out and the raw bane Jamaican in me will so come out.

I am not fake and I refuse to be fake to please anyone. Not even God I will be fake for.
I will not change me to please God or anyone. I have to be me because God never asked any of us to change ourselves. I am perfect the way he made me, you are perfect the way he made you. I truly love me and infinitely truly truly truly truly love him.

I know one good deed wipe out thousands of sins

That's a lie

It is the infinite truth but guess what what you do must be done out of truth and true love. *Not love but true love.*

Many of you have children do you want to see them fail?

No

So why are we failing them?

Hey you can hate me. Laugh at me. Ignore me. Tell me to kiss your ass because I am meddling in something that does not concern me. It is up to you but at the appointed time God's people must leave out of Babylon and find themselves home.

At the end of the day your destruction was predicted long before you were born and the book, man's book which is the devil's book must be fulfilled.

You don't have to look into what I say to see if it will work because the solutions to you are farfetched and to a lot of you I do not know what I am talking about.

Some are saying these are not solutions but a deranged person's way of selling books.

Whatever you are saying you have your opinion and you are entitled to them.

You know and other people know that America is going to fail. This was predicted yes by man and not God. You can change your future.

All I have to say is remember Eve she listened to the devil and she was kicked out of God's kingdom. She did die even though the devil told her she would not. He used her to get in meaning unleash chaos on the earth and she was left holding the bag. *He screwed her* and at the end of the day whether you the American public like it or not he is screwing you also. Like I have told you he is going to keep you fighting until you are bankrupt. All the oil and free money you were promised you will have none because at the end of the day the oil sands will be gone just like the glaciers and what then. You will have no money, no oil, nothing. *If he was not loyal to Eve how the hell is he going to be loyal to you?*

Look at it from another angle now. America goes bankrupt and it will if nothing is done to bring the debt load down.

Say you are bankrupt now, your green back will become worthless. Nobody is going to want your money because it has become so devalued it's useless. How many of you have money in a European bank account? Look at the Euro and Pound, the Canadian Dollar. Those currencies have a high monetary value. Right now where is the US Dollar sitting? Stay with me here for one minute. Yes with your money being devalued is good for some countries because now we can afford to buy your product. Your goods have become worthless no not worthless but penny stocks then. It's cheap. You still have a debt load of over 14 trillion dollars. If your money becomes worthless you will owe more than 14 trillion dollars because it will cost your government more because they are spending more to buy foreign currency to pay off their debt. Do you see where I am going with this? If I am explaining it wrong please Mr. Economist or Financial advisor fill in the holes and explain it correctly. Tell me something America if all of this happens what's going to happen to the

American public because if your currency gets devalued there is no way in hell you will be able to repay your debt and every American in America will be screwed. Your land will become desolate, worse than Africa because you will become BITCH NIGGAS TO SIN AND THE BABYLONIANS WOULD HAVE WON. Do you think the slavery that you put black people through is anything compared to what you will go through?

Yes this is the worst case scenario but think. Like I said if you love your country so much do something to help it because at the end of the day IT'S NOT THE COUNTRY TO BE BLAMED BUT THE PEOPLE AND WHO WE ELECT TO OFFICE; NOT JUST THE PRESIDENT BUT EVERY ELECTED OFFICIAL. I DON'T CARE WHICH PARTY YOU REPRESENT YOU ARE TO BLAME BECAUSE ALL OF YOU HELPED TO ESCALATE YOUR DEBT. Everyone is saying we did this meaning elected the President and he messed us up. He inherited the debt. Cut back on your damned spending. And for all of you who are knocking free health care well not free because you have to pay something for it. There is nothing wrong with it-free health care. Poor people have to go to the doctor too. They are humans. What if the shoe was on the other foot? Wait no I retract that because if your country default the shoe will be on the other foot and many of you rich people, upper middle class people will know what it is like to have nothing be poor.

Hey some of you Black Owners of football and basket ball teams Canada, Africa, Jamaica. Just look into it and for all of you that are now going to rush and buy gold I wouldn't do that if I were you. Remember the housing market and how it came crashing down do you not think the same will happen to gold eventually? Just food for thought because I am so not an economist nor can I predict the future and any given economist can blast me from here to eternity.

You all have your futures in your hand so do something to help your country and *PLEASE PEOPLE DO NOT GIVE ALL YOUR WORLDLY POSSESSIONS. IF YOU ONLY HAVE $1.00 PER MONTH TO GIVE, GIVE THE DOLLAR.*

DO NOT GIVE WHAT YOU DON'T HAVE.

- If anything comes out of this. Stop the blame game and help your President and Country to bring your debt load down. You owe him that much.

- You owe your country that much

- You owe your children and yourself that much

- You owe future generations that much

- More importantly you owe yourself and God that much.

7) The Environment

Man oh man does it irritate me to see everyone squabbling over the environment. CLEAN IT THE HELL UP. Stop bickering because the life you save will be your own.

Everyone thinking about the cost of cleaning up green house gases saying it is too costly. It's too costly but yet the profits you receive from your products sit well with you.

The earth is losing the battle – fight with

humans. It cannot sustain us nor will it be able to maintain us given our current state.

Given the amount of pollutants emitted in the air each day how can there be a balance. We cannot let the environment continue this way or we will eventually have none and we will all die. There has to be a balance in nature and if there isn't we will hit dire straits soon. We all want bigger and better like I've said but no one wants to clean.

The glaciers have receded so much in the last 100 years that none of us truly care because we keep emitting deadly carbons in the air carbons that come back down in the form of acid rain. As ordinary people we don't care and I say this loosely because the more we drive oil or gas driven cars the more pollutants they emit in the air. We have to curve our obsession with gasoline because it does have a significant impact on the environment. Gas companies what about plant based alternatives to fuel our cars. I don't know the process because like I said I know nothing of renewable energy you do and this should be your main focus.

Once the glaciers go what then? How will man sustain themselves because the core temperature of earth is rising each and every day?

If precipitation is decreasing more and more in some areas how will man be able to survive.

Will drought and famine not ravage the land even more?

How will developed nations fair with scarcity of food?

How will we cope with low to no adequate drinking water because this will affect our water supply worse than it is now?

What about diseases because man will not be able to ward off some of the diseases that are yet to come?

If none of you including the citizens of the world are thinking about the future how will we survive? More importantly for us that have children and grandchildren how will they survive?

It's not about us anymore it's about our children's and great grandchildren's future. We are screwing up ours why should we screw up theirs. What we do affect them in the long run and we cannot leave our burdens and messes on them. Many of you have children too and no matter the amount of money you accumulate it will not save you from death. We are all eventually going to die but we can prolong this by helping ourselves now. For some of us that are in cold countries in the spring and summer time take public transit more often and leave your cars at home. I know it is convenient but try to do your part by using public transit.

If the grocery store is in walking distance walk and take your kids that can push your buggy or carry grocery bags.

If laundry mat is in walking distance walk to the laundry mat. Now this would be incentive for someone to design sturdy laundry buggies with wheels and a separate compartment for liquid detergents and fabric softeners.

As ordinary citizens there are so much that we can do but every individual have to want change. We can't just rely on companies and government because at the end of the day we are consumers we buy these products and if the product is not environmentally friendly why buy them.

No matter what we do we cannot be totally pollutant free but we can do more to help the environment. We have to live with nature and the more we pollute it is the more we destroy it. The more we destroy it is the quicker we age and yes the quicker we die because all that we consume we are consuming pollutants whether it be in our water or the food that we eat.

And no people no food on the face of this planet is totally organic because the water that comes down from the heavens have pollutants in it.

When are we going to wake up and do for self and the environment? Tell me something people are we going to wake up when mutation of our genes become so altered that science can't do nothing to help.

Each and everyone one of us have to think and please no protesting because you don't need to protest. Well we do but not here. As a citizen do your part to help the environment. If you don't have to drive everywhere don't and please turn off the lights and don't leave them constantly on. I know we have kids and they are the number one offenders in my book for leaving the lights and their gaming systems on. Hey Sony how about this if the game system is left on for over an hour without play how about making the system go on stand bye or even shut off automatically. I know some television system does this but the newer models don't. How about designing newer model televisions like these?

Got to stop now because I am going over board and way beyond my knowledge.

Oh yea please forgive any typos and misspelling that you may find in this book. Oh Lord the verb confusion. Well forgive all grammatical errors okay.

As I close I dedicate Hold On by R. Kelly to you America. You now need to hold and truly do for you.

Michelle

Other books by Michelle Jean

Blackman Redemption – The Rise and Fall of Jamaica

Blackman Redemption – The Truth about God

Love Bound – Book 1 and Two

A Little Talk/A Time for Fun and Play

Dedication Unto My Kids

Behind the Scars

My Collective a Collection of Prayers Sayings and Poems

More Talk

My Collective the other side of me

My Collective the dark side of love